THE BALLAD OF
ROBERT EALEY

★ ★ ★ AND HIS ★ ★ ★

FIVE CARELESS LOVERS

Liz

We all have transformative experiences.

This was mine with music.

Once upon a time, this really happened in Fort Worth, Texas — Love,

THE BALLAD OF
ROBERT EALEY
★ ★ ★ ## AND HIS ★ ★ ★
FIVE CARELESS LOVERS

AN ORAL HISTORY AS TOLD BY

FREDDIE CISNEROS ★ SUMTER BRUTON
MIKE BUCK ★ JACKIE NEWHOUSE

by JOE NICK PATOSKI

HORNE & WELLESLEY PUBLISHERS

Joe Nick Patoski
Horne & Wellesley Publishers

Printed in the United States of America

Subjects: Fort Worth, Texas Blues, juke joints, Robert Ealey

Book and cover design by Nancy McMillen
Nancy McMillen Design, Austin, Texas

IN MEMORY OF
ROBERT EALEY

AND

THE REVEREND
GOOD ROCKIN'
RALPH OWENS

HOT DANCE TUNES

ROBERT EALEY

★ ★ ★ **AND HIS** ★ ★ ★

FIVE CARELESS
LOVERS
JUMPING THE BLUES FOR YOU

★ ★ ★ ★ ★ ★ ★ ★ ★

4 STRING JACK
LITTLE BUCKY
GOOD ROCKING RALPH
BE-BOP BRUTON
SO. OF THE BORDER SAMMY

IN 1971

in my hometown of Fort Worth, Texas, a band formed that changed my life.
It was a particularly musical time for a twenty-year-old kid. I
had left college and returned home to open a small record shop
on the bad side of town with a couple friends of mine, and work
as a disc jockey on KFAD-FM in Arlington, a station with very
spotty reception that paid $1.60 an hour—minimum wage—for
the pleasure of selecting good songs from an expansive library
of LP albums, and playing them on the radio, airing commer-
cials whenever they were scheduled. It was free-form radio at
its best, showcasing mostly new rock music, but with a heap-
ing helping of jazz and classic rhythm 'n' blues. On Sundays, a
guy who worked in an Arlington record shop would host a
blues show, as interpreted by British bands such as Pretty
Things and Led Zeppelin.

One day Mike Buck wandered into Natural Records, my
shop, from down the street, or maybe he came in through the
beaded curtain separating the record shop from the adjacent
head shop. The bonding was pretty quick. I sold records. He

Robert Ealey and His Five Careless Lovers, entertaining the crowd at Mable's Eat Shop.

1

"You really had to bear witness to Robert Ealey and His Five Careless Lovers in their element, meaning in a predominantly Black club in Fort Worth, where Robert functioned as both singer and master of ceremonies."

collected records, but not the kind I sold. The records Mike sought were well worn 45s, the little records from back in the 1950s and 1960s with the big hole in the middle, surrounded by the circular label, bearing the only text and (sometimes) art acknowledging the music. The records Mike played were crazy, mostly obscure blues, with a whole lot of rocking thrown in, most all of it from Texas. These weren't some faraway exotic sounds. This was local, music made from around here.

One night, I took up his invitation to come see his band, Robert Ealey and His Five Careless Lovers, who had started their weekend residency at Mable's Eat Shop, a one-room clapboard shack at the corner of Horne and Wellesley, the heart of Como, the Black community of Fort Worth's west side. Over the course of a couple hour-long sets, everything came together. The memory is a blur now, a collage of the singer cutting loose with a long unintelligible wail punctuated at the end by the guttural fuzz of a harmonica (or what sounded like a harmonica), electric guitars clanging, snare drum and cymbals thrashing, church organ and bass somehow carving out a shuffle from the chaos, all performed in front of maybe 30 folks, most of them Black, practically all laughing and yelling above the din.

That was the moment, right there. The world of music I'd grown up in and been accustomed to—rock, soul, radio, concerts, theaters, arenas—peeled back, revealing itself as a business: an enticing, seductive enterprise, mind you, one that has held my attention for most of my writing life, but a business nonetheless.

What I experienced at Mable's, and later at the New Blue Bird across the street, and at other venues where Robert Ealey and His Five Careless Lovers played, was music as art, made for all the wrong/right reasons. It was honest, direct, rocking, intense, mesmerizing, communal, personal, uplifting, and insane—all at once.

The experience did not translate easily.

The album *Robert Ealey and His Five Careless Lovers Live at the New Blue Bird Nite Club* was too raw and too primitive for FM album rock radio. The band bruised easily when traveling—Austin audiences into Stevie and Jimmie Vaughan wondered what the big deal was. You really had to bear witness to Robert Ealey and His Five Careless Lovers in their element, meaning in a predominantly Black club in Fort

Worth, where Robert functioned as both singer and master of ceremonies. He understood how the whole room was the stage, knew how to work the audience while he sang from a distance and close up, moving from table to table, tantalizing the patrons, when to walk the bar or the pool table to really work up the crowd, when to bring on guest performers, and how to run the whole show.

This was genuine Texas blues, the hometown stuff those British bands had been stealing from and sending back to American youth for the past decade. Only unlike the Brits, this was the real deal, skipping along a gliding rhythm called the Fort Worth Shuffle.

Ain't seen anything like it since.

The band at Mable's Eat Shop. From left: Good Rockin' Ralph Owens, Sumter Bruton, Mike Buck, Freddie Cisneros, Robert Ealey, and Jackie Newhouse.

In exchange for that gift, I offer this ballad of that band, Robert Ealey and His Five Careless Lovers, as told in the words of the four surviving members of the ensemble that turned my head around, and opened my ears for good. These interviews were conducted over the course of the first half of 2020 at the homes of Sumter Bruton and Mike Buck; with Freddie Cisneros, over the phone and at Record Town in Fort Worth; with Jackie Newhouse at Giddyup's Bar near his South Austin residence, and on the couch at Record Town. Johnny Reno, Craig Simecheck, Michael Pellecchia, and Gerard Daily also chimed in.

–JNP

> **"My sister had a friend who would bring over John Lee Hooker and Jimmy Reed albums. That's where I started. Family is where it came from."**

FIRST RUMBLINGS

Freddie: My brother and sister were bringing home Fats Domino, Little Richard, Chuck Berry, and Bo Diddley albums. They were seven or eight years older than me. "Yes! This is it!" And from there, "Where did this come from?" My sister had a friend who would bring over John Lee Hooker and Jimmy Reed albums. That's where I started. Family is where it came from.

[On his first band] I started out on drums. I would provide the rhythm for whatever these guys wanted to play. My first gig was at a bar. Me and my friends played the gig, and at the end of the night, the owner had left. We didn't get paid. One of the guys in the band knew the owner, and he was real embarrassed. I went home and was unloading my drums about two in the morning, and here comes my dad in a taxicab, and he falls out of this taxicab just drunk as a skunk. He said, "How'd the gig go, son?" I made the mistake of saying we didn't get paid. He got pissed, man, and he went in the house, got a butcher knife, and said, "Let's go." We went to the bar owner's house—here's this drunk Mexican beating on the door with this butcher knife. "Where's my son's money?" Lights are coming on all over the neighborhood. It was like a Mexican ATM, man, these five- and ten-dollar bills coming out from underneath the door. So, we got paid. That was my first gig.

My first record was with some country guy who needed a drummer over at Manco Studios, out there in White Settlement. Jim Jones and the Chaunteys [a popular teen rock band in the mid-1960s] were the first I can remember recording with. We went down to Houston [to record for Huey P. Meaux], and Jim Jones' mom, she kept telling us, "Now, don't eat or drink anything this guy gives you."

After Jim Jones and the Chaunteys, I met a fella named Leon Ellis—Leon Ellis and the Emeralds—and we played around

Jim Jones (middle) and the Chaunteys with Freddie Cisneros (lower right).

town a bunch. Leon would take me to this place called Rayford's to hear U.P. Wilson playing, and Robert [Ealey] was playing drums back then [as the Boogie Chillen Boys, U.P. and Robert's duo that dates back to the 1950s]. This had to have been '66 or '65. I just loved it, man. I couldn't get enough of it.

[Robert Ealey was born in Texarkana in 1925, and moved to Dallas in 1951 to pursue a career in gospel music. He got distracted by Lil' Son Jackson, Frankie Lee Sims, Mercy Baby and other Dallas bluesmen, and became a bluesman himself, playing drums with U.P. Wilson and with other bands after moving to Fort Worth where his daytime job was driving a truck for Bruce Alford Lumber and Door.]

Freddie: I started hitting all these Black bars like Gentry's on Rosedale and hearing all these people. They were so friendly to me. By then, I was playing some guitar with Jim.

That's when I joined Reverend Filmore [and the Swinging Flames]. Man, that was the coolest bunch of guys I ever met. The way they dressed—when they played, we wore tuxes and iridescent suits. It was just so cool. *Every one* of them was a ladies' man. I did a lot of growing up. Yeah, man.

I would just hang out with them. Being on the inside with that group of people, I got insight on what they were up against. "Well, no, we can't go there. Because, well . . ." They stayed out of certain parts of town, and they just kinda flew under the radar. And I flew under the radar with them. I got insight into how life was.

One of the few Black people that they'd allow in The Cellar [a storied after-hours club, with other Cellars in Dallas and Houston] was Reverend Filmore and the band. They knew who he was, and they let him in, him and Ray Sharpe and Freddie King. But it was pretty racist back then. They had a sign said, "The

Reverend Filmore (left) and the Swinging Flames, with Freddie Cisneros (far right), along with Ray Cleveland (second from left).

highest cover charge in the world," like $100,000 or something [the doorman would point to the sign if a Black person tried to come inside]. It was just awful.

One Saturday, they came and picked me up—Reverend and Ray and Joe—and we went to the movies over there at the Tivoli. It was a Western, and it was the noisiest crowd I've ever been around. Every time one of these cowboys would get an arrow in him, they'd be like, "You motherfucker!" "*Die*, you honky motherfucker!" I couldn't believe it, man. It was just an experience, seeing everything from the inside out.

Back in the '60s when I was playing with Reverend Filmore, we'd hit the Blue Bird, and we'd hit a place on Rosedale called Beaver's. That was across the street from the Good Luck hamburger place. We'd play Gentry's over

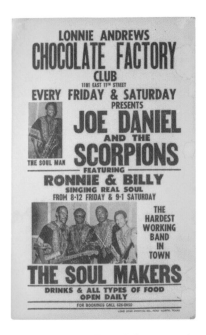

Poster advertising Lonnie Andrews' Chocolate Factory, one of scores of Black clubs around Fort Worth in the early 1970s featuring live bands.

Advertising poster for Black blues musicians Ray Flangin and King Earl.

there on Rosedale. One night I was unpacking my guitar, taking it out of my car. It was dark and there were guys standing in front of Gentry's. They came over to me. They thought I was breaking into cars. And finally, one of them said, "No, no, man, I know him. He plays the music." That let me off the hook, but man, they were ready to kill me, thinking I was some guy out there trying to steal tires. Once I got established in some of those bars, everybody knew me. I could go in any of those places and feel safe.

We played a gig in Frederick, Oklahoma, and we were billed as Johnnie Taylor, and we pulled it off, playing "Part Time Love" and a few other tunes.

Sumter was doing the same thing I was doing back in high school, listening to these cool bands, like Ray Sharpe, hitting all these clubs, going to Rayford's and Gentry's. It was kinda like "Animal House." If you wanted to get entertained, you'd go to the Black end of town. That's where the really good entertainment was. When we had a party or a dance in high school [Class of '66, Paschal High School], you'd have a Black band. That was the thing to do. That's how I met Little Al Ford. He had a band called the Hi-Fi's.

Sumter: I started listening to blues and boogie-woogie records when I was three [his parents owned Record Town, a record shop across the street from Texas Christian University]. I couldn't read, but I knew the colors and labels I liked—[the ones with] Charlie Parker, Miles Davis, Pete Johnson, Joe Turner. I didn't like Stan Kenton.

My dad would say, "Don't ever call a Black person a n----r. Ever." He said they can call themselves that, but you don't do it. He played with a 14-piece Black band when he was 14, in Philadelphia. "How'd you get that gig?" He said, "I had a car and a set of drums."

After going to [Sunday] Mass, we'd go down to the Mexican Inn downtown, then my dad would take us on a tour of East Fourth Street and all the south side and show us places. He knew about them. He was a musician. He was playing on Jacksboro Highway.

First time I saw blues was at a fraternity rush party. Little Al and the Hi-Fi's were playing on the roof of L.D. Bell on Montgomery Street, and I was mesmerized. Al played a Fender Telecaster left-handed. I'd been listening to blues, but hadn't seen anything but jazz bands. That's what my dad played. I went home that night and told [brother] Stephen, "I'm gonna learn how to play guitar."

He loaned me one of his guitars, but he only taught me two chords. He wouldn't teach me the third chord. "How do you resolve the blues thing?"

"You gotta learn that on your own." Well, I did. Bobby Bland, B.B. King, Kats Karavan and Jim Lowe [on WRR radio in Dallas, which featured blues], KNOK played blues all day, Doctor Jazzbo on KRZY 730 played blues all the time. "Lay it on the table, Mabel, because I am able!" They were out of Grand Prairie. John R. was on WLAC in Nashville. I'd drive my car to Waco and back listening to him [at night]. It came in real good out of town. I used to tape Wolfman Jack on the X border radio station on my Ampeg tape recorder.

I had records already, so I just started listening. Brother Jack McDuff, early Miles Davis, Dexter Gordon—they were all blues players to me. When I was real young, I'd ride my bicycle over to the Blue Bird and listen through the walls. There were five blues clubs within blocks of each other on Camp Bowie [Boulevard, the main drag in west Fort Worth]—all white boys, like Delbert's band, the Ron-Dels.

After seeing Little Al, I started going to T.J.'s Chicken in the Basket and going to [other Black] places. I sat in with Freddie King one night at Chicken in the Basket for a wedding, a white wedding.

I was in the Air Force Reserve and my best friends were Black guys. One night, I took one of my good friends—he was from Roxbury near Boston—to the Casa Del Sol, a private club where my dad had played. I knew the manager there. We were turned away at the door. I was real embarrassed. We ended up going to T.J.'s Chicken in the Basket.

Cornell Dupree was real good, and Ray Sharpe was really good, but I listened to B.B. King, and T-Bone Walker was my man. I liked Barney Kessel, Herb Ellis.

Mike: I grew up typical—the Stones and the Beatles, the Christmas of '64, when everybody got either a guitar or a drum kit. The Stones led to looking: "Who's McDaniels? Who's Morganfield?"—all that. I was checking out the old guys, and there was the English blues-rock. We were kinda doing that, kind of a Stones-Yardbirds thing with different

> "First time I saw blues was at a fraternity rush party. Little Al and the Hi-Fi's were playing on the roof of L.D. Bell on Montgomery Street, and I was mesmerized. Al played a Fender Telecaster left-handed."

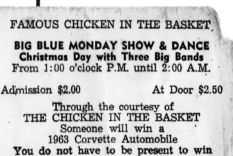

FAMOUS CHICKEN IN THE BASKET

BIG BLUE MONDAY SHOW & DANCE
Christmas Day with Three Big Bands
From 1:00 o'clock P.M. until 2:00 A.M.

Admission $2.00   At Door $2.50

Through the courtesy of
THE CHICKEN IN THE BASKET
Someone will win a
1963 Corvette Automobile
You do not have to be present to win

Nᵒ 0510

"I met Freddie at this big hippie house over off Eighth Avenue in the Magnolia-Rosedale area, on Alston Street. He was on the way out and I was on the way in. He was into Freddie King and all this stuff, and we kinda started playing."

bands I'd play in. We never played anywhere outside the garage much, maybe an occasional YMCA gig.

One afternoon in 1970, I was driving on the freeway and I saw Ike and Tina's bus, so I followed it to this hotel downtown. The band all got out, and they were all the worse for wear. Seemed like Ike and Tina were having a fight. They were kinda over by themselves. I started talking to the band, and they were "Anything for the head?" I took them all down to Trinity Park, that hippie hangout. These guys are walking around with their do-rags and their continental clothes and shit amongst all these hippies, like Funkadelic had landed there in a spaceship, bought a bunch of acid, pot. We all took acid, the band and me and my girlfriend. We went to their show that night at the Guys and Dolls [Ballroom]. It was pretty nuts.

I met Freddie [Cisneros] at this big hippie house over off Eighth Avenue in the Magnolia-Rosedale area, on Alston Street. He was on the way out and I was on the way in. He was into Freddie King and all this stuff, and we kinda started playing. I'd been going to Record Town for years, and Sumter had been preaching the gospel to me about the blues guys Gatemouth Brown and T-Bone Walker.

There was this crazy guitar player named Pete. He was kind of a hillbilly but he liked blues, and he knew Jackie. He was from this little hillbilly neighborhood tucked away in there east of I-35 by Seminary Drive. Jackie and all the other guys called it Ignorant Hill. That's where this guy Pete was from [he was a neighbor friend of Jackie's]. We were trying to back up this guy Pete, but he played really loud and kinda out of control. It was fun for a little bit.

Jackie: There was always music in the house. My dad's father played the homemade fiddle that he'd made himself, at barn dances up in Fannin County. My mother was a Baptist preacher's daughter, and she played piano. We had a piano in the house. The Beatles on the Ed Sullivan Show in 1964 changed everything. I was 11 and I had a grade-school friend named Pete Hooper who played a little guitar. I think we did the fifth- and sixth-grade talent shows at Carter Park Elementary. We were the only ones that didn't lip-synch the Beatles. We actually got up there and sang and played instruments.

Pete moved away. I didn't see him until my senior year at O.D. Wyatt High School. He moved back to the neighborhood and showed up. He had a Fender Bandmaster and a Gibson Les

Jackie "4 String Jack" Newhouse performing with Mike Buck and Freddie Cisneros at TJ's Chicken in the Basket. Mike would pick up Jackie at high school and drive him to the gig.

Paul Junior. He plugged it in and whipped off "Going Home" by Ten Years After. He was that good and that fast and that powerful a guitar player. I had an old Kay bass sitting around at the house, so we started jamming. He said, "Hey, I know this drummer named Mike Buck." So, that's how I got to know Mike.

The problem with Pete was that as good of a player as he was—and he could have been as good or better than just about anybody that I've played with—he couldn't play in public. He would just freeze up and forget everything he knew. We used to pester the guys at The Cellar to let us sit in. We got there early one day and there was nobody to play, so they finally said, "OK, y'all get up there." We played, and Pete completely forgot what he was doing. You know, we're trying to do a shuffle and he's—no changes, he was just soloing like crazy, and basically, at that point, Mike was real pissed. They pulled the plug on us halfway through the first song.

BUCK AND JACKIE AND FREDDIE

||||||||||||||||||||||||||||||||||||||||||||||||||||||||

Jackie: Freddie had just gotten out of the Army and back from Vietnam. What Freddie saw in us, I have no idea. We could barely play. After we found out who he was, he was like a god. He played with Jim Jones and the Chaunteys. On the south side of Fort Worth, they were *the* band. Freddie was my first mentor. He really taught me not just how to play, but how to be a musician, how to behave onstage, and how to carry yourself.

I was working at Zeke's Fish and Chips at the time, and my manager went to school with Freddie, and he told me, "Freddie, he's a blues guy. He's not gonna play this rock stuff." I said, "We know." Mike was heavy into collecting blues records, and he was showing me the roots of where Eric Clapton and Jeff Beck and all these guys were coming from, playing me Freddie King records.

Frosty [drummer Barry Smith] told me that when Freddie King came along, it caused a schism between guitar players. There were the Howard Roberts-Joe Pass guys, and then there were the new guys that embraced Freddie King. Freddie King was really a game-changer.

We were looking for a singer because me and Mike and Freddie didn't sing. We all knew Sumter from Record Town. That was the one record store we *didn't* steal from. Sumter was playing out in Rendon with Robert, Johnny B. [Searcy], and Ralph. [The ensemble was alternately known as Johnny and the Mustangs, and Robert and the Tornados, according to Mike Price, who documented the group with the recording *Blues That Time Forgot*.] Somehow, we ended up [joining them and] driving out to Pilot Point, Texas, to do a gig at another juke joint run by a DPS officer—he was there in full uniform, keeping the peace. Robert was the drummer, and Ralph was on keyboards. We went with the three-guitar lineup, but Johnny B. eventually dropped out. Robert moved to the front with Bucky on drums. We became the Five Careless Lovers and ended up playing every Friday and Saturday at Mable's Eat Shop.

T.J.'S CHICKEN IN THE BASKET

||||||||||||||||||||||||||||||||||||||||||||||||

Jackie: Mike and I were just driving around the east side one day, probably over near Rosedale and Riverside, and we saw a placard on a telephone pole for Freddie King playing at T.J.'s Chicken in the Basket [the biggest club among a strip of Black clubs along East Fourth Street in the Trinity River bottoms, with a stage and palm trees painted on the walls. They made note of the date and went to the show]. It wasn't like the hippie places that we went to. These people were in their suits and their best clothes, jewels. It had a real stage. Little Al and the Hi-Fi's, the house band, were backing him up. It was kinda scary going in. We were made to feel very welcome.

Freddie King with Little Al and the Hi-Fi's at T.J.'s Chicken in the Basket (Mike Buck on right in photo at far left).

Sumter: Freddie King was smart. He'd play a lot of frat parties, and he'd book himself at a Black club in the same town as the frat party. He'd do 40 minutes at a TCU frat party with white guys backing him up, drive himself over to T.J.'s and play 40 minutes with Little Al and the Hi-Fi's, then drive back to the TCU area to play another set at the frat party. Instead of making $200 a night, he made $400.

Mike: Freddie King was playing [at T.J.'s Chicken in the Basket], and we went to see him. I guess we just started talking to T.J. "We've got a band." "Oh yeah? You boys come on by, and you can play Monday afternoons."

The Blue Monday matinee was before the other [headlining] bands would come on, usually Little Al and the Hi-Fi's. We met a bunch of crazy people. This guy named Woody Reese had just gotten out of the federal penitentiary for forgery, and he had this hooker sister who would come around. She became enamored of Ted Tucker [a blues-collector friend of the band].

Jackie: I'd get out of school and we'd drive over there and just be jamming, and Freddie [Cisneros] would show up, and different people from the neighborhood would come by and sit in. I guess it was more just like a blues jam. He'd pay us a couple of dollars, maybe five bucks each. One time he gave us $2 and a bottle of T-Bird. I think we were a novelty, yeah.

Mike: A lot of the neighborhood people would come in and drink and hang out. I remember one night we played and T.J. gave us a dollar and a bottle of wine. Not a dollar apiece, a dollar. But we got all the chicken and all the booze we could drink, and wine. It was an incredible learning experience, just all the cats that would come by and play, different guys would come around from Little Al and the Hi-Fi's and Joe Daniel and the Scorpions. Little Al and the Hi-Fi's were the house band. They had horns. Whenever somebody'd come to town, like Freddie King, or Z.Z. Hill, they would back him up. We'd end up hanging out for their set after our set, and meeting more and more locals.

Freddie: T.J. was kind of the head man on Fourth Street. He had the biggest club. He was the guy to know if you wanted to do anything. Next door was Mrs. Allen's Silver Dollar. Those were the two big attractions right there. It was such a

Little Al and the Hi-Fi's, the band who turned Sumter Bruton on to live blues, were the house band at T.J.'s Chicken in the Basket and provided support to touring Chitlin' Circuit musicians, including Freddie King.

"It wasn't like the hippie places that we went to. These people were in their suits and their best clothes, jewels. It had a real stage."

11

> "It was the poorest neighborhood I've ever been in. But you go over there, and you were somebody. That was his slogan: 'Everybody's somebody at Chicken in the Basket.'"

depressed area. It was the poorest neighborhood I've ever been in. But you go over there, and you were somebody. That was his slogan: "Everybody's somebody at Chicken in the Basket." You go in there and get a beer, and you were somebody. It was an escape for those folks, man. They really needed it. It was bad.

Back in the '60s, when I was with Reverend Filmore, we hit a bunch of bars that I never would have known about. And then I just started exploring on my own. Mike and Jack and myself, we'd just play anywhere for fun and the excitement.

Jackie: A guy named Woody Reese [pictured at right] took us under his wing. He had just gotten out of the pen. I don't know what his deal was. He was a hustler, maybe a street-level drug dealer. I don't know. He played a little guitar and bass, sat in with us, and looked over us and protected us. They called that neighborhood The Bottoms.

Mike: The club had these little Chinaman paintings, music notes painted on the wall, a sign: "We have fun, but no guns," and the club's motto: "Everybody's somebody, even old T.J."

Mrs. Allen's, the Silver Dollar next door, was more lowdown than Chicken in the Basket, which was relatively upscale because they had the Chitlin' Circuit big names play there. But it was still lowdown. Silver Dollar was great. Mrs. Allen, she'd be at the door, and she looked like she was asleep all the time, but she had her little gun nearby. You could always buy half a pint of gin or whatever from her on Sunday, any time, night or day. She plied us with that, and we started playing over there. We started playing a bunch of little clubs. J.D. King had another club next door to her that we played, and other clubs around Fort Worth, like on Evans Avenue, Sugar Hill.

Famous Chicken In The Basket
DINE and DANCE
Where Everybody Is Somebody -
Even Down To Old T. J. and Lois Burgers
335-0250
1908 E. 4th St.   Fort Worth, Texas 76102
See T. J. For Your Next Car

This one woman who ran a club had a big crush on Freddie. Tried to buy him cars. "I *love* Freddie."

Freddie: The lady that owned the place just fell in love with me, man. She had me on the pool table, trying to pin me down and dry hump me right there. *"Come on, honey."*

Mike: At one time we were called the South Side Blues Bombers or something like that, but we never had a proper name. You know, it was mainly for fun, although we were serious about it.

THE HOP

||||||||||||||||||||||||||||||||||||

Freddie: After the [Vietnam] war, I was trying to find myself, and I was hanging out at The HOP [the acronym for the House of Pizza on Berry Street, a popular beer bar hangout for college students at Texas Christian University that featured live bands, including local blues players]. I lived on that side of town. Bucky was doing dishes. Robert and Sumter were playing. I met Jackie through Mike, and we all hit it off. Mike was a record collector. I had records, but I never thought of myself as a collector. He turned me on to a lot of stuff.

Mike: The HOP was the scene for Sumter and his crowd. They'd go there every day and drink. They had their tables, little cliques. Somehow, I guess through Sumter, I got a job washing dishes at The HOP.

Sumter: I met Robert Ealey at The HOP through Joe Murph. Me and Joe Murph and [Sumter's brother] Stephen and a drummer played a pickup gig with Robert. Joe Murph was friends with Robert. Joe was the only white kid to graduate from Como High

School. Robert stayed in touch with me and called me one night and said, "Sumter, do you play bass?" "Sure!" "I've got a job tonight in Arlington." I had to go to his house on East Shaw and followed him to this place in downtown Arlington [Jack's Country Boys Place]. Johnny B. [Searcy] was there, and we started playing together.

Playing with Robert wasn't my first professional job, but close to it. I was still in the Air Force Reserve when we started together [1968]. Some of the guys with me in the reserves would come out and hear us play.

The beginnings of the band at The HOP, The House of Pizza, the small joint on Berry Street near the TCU campus where Sumter Bruton first met Robert Ealey.

13

JOHNNY B'S

||||||||||||||||||||||||||||||||||||||||||||||||

Sumter: We played every Saturday night at Johnny B.'s Old Country Inn in Rendon. You go to Rendon, then cross the railroad tracks and down into a little valley. The ice machine didn't work so they'd ice down the beer in the trunk of a car. The clientele was Mexican and Black with the [white] plantation owner who owned the property coming by every now and then to make sure everyone was having a good time.

Mike: The club was a little shack, a little country shack, this little juke joint.

Freddie: That was really, *really* down-home. There was no bathroom in the club. There was a real outhouse. They didn't sell beer. You bought everything at the liquor store next door or a little grocery store. Me and Bucky and Robert were playing with Johnny B., and man, this place was just a little *house*, is all it was, and all of a sudden, people started shooting. And it was just like Vietnam all over. I dove under the pool table. So did Mike. I grabbed my guitar and said, "Let's get the hell outta here," and we did. We left his drums there and my amp and everything else.

The next day, Mike and I went to see if we could get our stuff, and there's Johnny B. in there drinking a beer. "Hey, fellas, where'd you go last night?" "Shit, man, what happened? How many people got killed?" He said, "Oh, they all missed. Nobody got hurt." It was all point blank. There must have been seven or eight guns going off. He said, "Where did you go? We had another set to do."

Mike: We were hiding out in Barbara Logan's van. People were all running around and milling around in the parking lot and guns going off, and people yelling and laughing. It was a really surreal scene.

Sumter: Ralph and me and Robert were playing together. I knew Mike and I knew Freddie. I didn't know Jackie yet. They had a singer, kinda like what we were doing, 'cept we were more popular. I knew Freddie from House of Pizza and I knew Mike from the record store and coming over to my house. He and Ted [Tucker] would come over. I'd play them records. I had the biggest collection in town at the time. We just got together, started playing. The other band broke up. Just happened.

Mike Buck learned how to drum by watching Robert Ealey play, then took over the drum chair when Robert stepped out front to sing lead.

Mike: [On learning drums from Robert] Just watching him play that crazy jungle thing he would do. He would go out and front the band [to sing, occasionally], so I started playing drums behind him. I would sit in. Finally, I just started being the drummer, and then I brought Freddie and Jackie in, because we'd been playing together in this other band.

Sumter: Mike and Freddie and them, they all played the blues, and me and Robert and Ralph, we all liked the same stuff, and they knew more songs than Johnny B. did. Johnny played kind of fast and slow, blues and shuffle.

MABLE'S EAT SHOP

||||||||||||||||||||||||||||||||||||||||||||||||||||||||||||||||||||||||||||

Sumter: You know where downtown Como was—four blocks from the Blue Bird and the corner of Horne and Wellesley. There was a theater, a grocery, and a bunch of clubs. Across Horne Street from the Blue Bird was Mable's Eat Shop. That's where the Careless Lovers started playing [in 1971]. It was a dump. Mable lived right there in the first house, catty-cornered to Mable's. Mable Everhart was a character. She was married to a guy with big bug eyes, only they weren't married anymore, but they were working together. Mable's didn't have any hot water, so they had to boil the water. It was great fried chicken. Many a night I got saved. I didn't have the money. I got five pieces of chicken. Oh, God, that was good chicken.

They couldn't pass any health inspections.

There was a room in there. It was a bathroom that you didn't go into, had a towel over the door. That's where 24-hours-a-day gambling went on, throwing dice. Never had any problems come out of that room. People walked out of there, I'm sure, broke. It was a little room, only fit about six people in there. They threw dice all the time. We usually didn't go back there.

[One night] I left my amplifier onstage. And next morning, Saturday morning, I go back. I said, "Shit, I hope it's here." Walk on in. The fuckin' door's wide open. Amp's sitting there. My jacket's sitting on top of it. And the boys back in the back, they were shooting craps. I peeked my head in, said, "I'm just here to get my amplifier." That was it. They never even looked at the amplifier.

Mike: Mable had this husband named Eris. He'd always fix us fried chicken and take care of us. He had this really raggedy dog named Robert Johnson, had all these scars on him, always getting in fights. He could climb trees. He could climb over fences, little short-legged dog,

Freddie: Mable's Eat Shop was tore down, man. It was good eats. She could fry some chicken. I liked hers better than T.J.'s, to be honest with you. It was mainly a restaurant, if you want to call it that; it was just a shack. It was real limited everything. "Got Budweiser?" "No." "Got Pearl?" "No." If you got a chicken sandwich it was a piece of bread on a plate with half a chicken

> "Mable's didn't have any hot water, so they had to boil the water. It was great fried chicken. Many a night I got saved. I didn't have the money. I got five pieces of chicken. Oh, God, that was good chicken."

Robert playing his harmonica, sans harmonica, with the Five Careless Lovers laying down the groove behind him at Mable's Eat Shop while being filmed for a documentary.

> "During the day it was dominoes and beer and music. The jukebox was always blasting. They had a big refrigerator with lots of beer. They could accommodate a full house."

on top of it. It was a small place. There was no ID check. They didn't even consider that, man. It was just—if you came in there, you could drink. I mean, it didn't matter how old you were.

Sumter: Things were scarier over on the south side at Sugar Hill. But the people out there in Como, I knew a lot of them. Same people came in. We started getting the Country Day kids and Trinity Valley kids. All my friends were coming out there. And we were all still pretty young. Probably wasn't as many white folks as the Blue Bird got, but there was a pretty good scattering of white kids at Mable's. Thirty people, and it was packed.

THE NEW BLUE BIRD

Sumter: We moved to the Blue Bird [in 1972] because Robert knew the people that ran it, Hiawatha and his wife, and they were good people.

Freddie: The Blue Bird was run a little better. Robert and Hiawatha were good friends. During the day it was dominoes and beer and music. The jukebox was always blasting. They had a big refrigerator

The New Blue Bird at the corner of Horne and Wellesley streets in Como.

with lots of beer. They could accommodate a full house. If there was a full house at Mable's, she would get overwhelmed and get pissed off.

Sumter: The Blue Bird had been the only jazz club in Como. They were booking jazz in the forties and fifties, R&B and honking and all that stuff. It fell on harder times. And then we went in there and got it back on its feet. It's still a dump, but it was nicer. It was a step up from Mable's.

Mike: It was a step across the street.

REPERTOIRE

||||||||||||||||||||||||||||||||||||||||||||||

Sumter: Some of it was requests. If we could play it, we'd try it. Robert would call one. We knew what he was talking about. There was no bandleader.

Mike: "Boogie Chillen," that was a big crowd-pleaser. "Turn on Your Love Light." We were doing pretty much standards, some other stuff thrown in for flavor, and of course a pretty unique interpretation, any way you look at it. It's not like we were playing it just like the records.

Freddie: Ralph would always do a little segment where he would do Fats Domino's

The move from Mable's Eat Shop across Horne Street to the New Blue Bird was a step up for Robert Ealey and His Five Careless Lovers.

"Blueberry Hill" or sometimes Ralph would sing "Walking With Frankie," by Frankie Lee Sims. He did it pretty often. That was definitely part of the [band] repertoire.

[Freddie's spotlight songs included Elmore James's "Pickin' the Blues," the Ray Sharpe classics "My Baby's Gone" and "Monkey's Uncle," and "There'll Be A Day" by Jimmy Reed. Sumter sang and played lead on B.B. King's "You Upset Me Baby," T-Bone Walker's "T-Bone Shuffle," and Gatemouth Brown's "Okie Dokie Stomp."]

19

ROBERT

||||||||||||||||||||||||||||||||

Freddie: Robert would just sing whatever Robert sang. Sometimes there were syllables that were not part of the song. He was always on the mark, and his voice was fabulous, but when it came down to exact words or lyrics, it didn't matter. He was more like an instrument than a vocalist.

Mike: Robert was easy to work with. He was a powerful singer. He could really belt it out. But he didn't really know the words, so he kinda made up words or kinda mumbled something. That was frustrating. That might have been one of the reasons the band split. He wouldn't really learn the song. I guess that's an art in itself. He did the "human harmonica" thing, and all that. But for a while we wanted something a little more.

He came up with Frankie Lee Sims and Mercy Baby and all those guys. He claims, and I've never seen any actual documentation on it, but he said on those early Frankie Lee Sims records, he plays like a washtub bass on it. Like on "Lucy Mae Blues." Not the band version he recorded later in Mississippi, but the early one recorded in Dallas. [The record] sounds like a washtub bass, no real notes or anything, just this sound. He always said that was him. I guess it could be.

He came from the country. Robert was talking about one gig they drove to in Waco and he forgot his drumsticks, so he cut some tree branches and was using those. Very resourceful.

[He engaged audiences with a rambling rap—"Twenty-four hours a day, we thinking about the blues." "If you understand the blues, give me a call." "When it's five o clock in the morning, and your car won't start, that's the blues!" "Give the drummer some, he ain't never had none."]

Freddie: As long as I played with Robert and these guys, there was never a rehearsal. We never rehearsed. Sometimes we'd just start a vamp or just do-doot, do-doot, and Robert would come in and make up a song, and that was it. Mostly syllables. Really, I mean syllables. I've got a recording of him doing "Cherry Pink and Apple Blossom White."

GOOD ROCKIN' RALPH

||||||||||||||||||||||||||||||||||||||||||||||||||||||||||||||||||||||||||||||

Sumter: Ralph worked for the railroad, had a good job, and he was a scratch golfer. He could shoot a 72. He'd shoot cross-handed and

Keyboardist Good Rockin' Ralph Owens gave the Five Careless Lovers their musical groove.

shoot like a motherfucker, you know. He was a good golfer. Down by the Water Department [just west of downtown] there was a bunch of Black clubs down there. The help lived down at the bottom. [Ralph and Sumter] played a couple of clubs down there with U.P., who was always coming down there. There was one club left. It was a neat little club.

Mike: Ralph was a little different. He was a churchgoing man. He didn't drink. He didn't curse. He didn't smoke or anything. He was real quiet. He always had a young girlfriend. She'd sit right up there by the stage.

The only thing I know about his previous history is he was in a band called the Brown Beatles that wore Beatle wigs. And he was a very religious guy, went to church, but he didn't take any shit off anybody. He was a strong guy. I remember me or Jackie would playfully, drunkenly razz him and he'd be on you, "What'd you say?" He wasn't preachy about it, or try to force it on anyone. It's that dichotomy like Jerry Lee—God and the devil. Ralph played at Robert's funeral, played organ. He might have spoken, too, as a preacher. I think he'd become a full reverend by then.

JOHNNY B. SEARCY

||||||||||||||||||||||||||||||||||||||||||||||||||||||||||||||||||||||||||||||

Freddie: Johnny B. would play with us from time to time. His tone was like a mosquito. I mean, it was just so harsh. But he made it work. I don't know—back then, you could buy those Japanese guitars for twenty bucks in a pawn shop, and that's what he had. With the rhythm section, it really sounded good. It really cut through. It was ear-splitting treble, but yeah, he was good. I'd been playing the clubs, and got used to following somebody that doesn't have any structure. They'd just go

21

Dueling guitarists Johnny B. Searcy (left) and Sumter Bruton with Robert Ealey on drums.

out and blow, man, and you'd have to watch them real close. And they might change in the middle of a progression; they'd just take off and you've just gotta follow them. John Lee Hooker was that way. He would just go to a IV chord when you're not expecting it, and it's like, "Oh, O.K." You just have to go slow; you can't force him to play, you know.

Johnny B. could put treble on top of treble. He knew how to control it, and he knew when not to play. And he had a great sense of rhythm.

Jackie: A lot of times, if he didn't know the chord, he would do the scratch thing to keep the rhythm, just mute the strings and scratch. His soloing was primitive Hound Dog Taylor-type, raw.

Mike: He was very rhythmic, you know. You just kinda go with it.

U.P. WILSON

Freddie: I met him before I went in the service back in the '60s. I saw him and Robert playing, the two of them, at Rayford's. Rayford's was on Rosedale, past Gentry's. U.P. played one-hand guitar, smoked a cigarette while he was doing it. Like it was two different people, you know. Really entertaining. I could kinda understand how to do it, but his hands were so massive, huge hands.

CATMAN FLEMING

Freddie: Catman Fleming was a real good friend of mine from the clubs over there on the east side. Catman was the coolest guy. He would tell me stories about Frankie Lee [Sims], but I never met him.

Mike: He was the first [Black musician] I hung out and socialized with. Sitting in my car, smoking a joint with him one time, he started singing "Marked Deck." I'd never heard it before—Mercy Baby and Frankie Lee Sims. I looked it up and found it, and later brought it to the T-Birds. We recorded a version of it. I got that from Catman. He'd show up, play bass, some guitar. No case on his guitar, cord wrapped around it, sometimes wearing one of those big ornamental sombreros. He was good. I mean, really primitive.

I always wanted to record him. In fact, we did a recording. It was ill-fated. I'd been hanging around Johnny Carroll a little at that time and recorded with him, and somehow convinced him that he owed me a favor. "OK. Come to the studio. We'll record something." I took Catman, Ralph, Freddie, Lou Ann [Barton], and a sax player. We recorded six or seven songs. But Johnny was really drunk, and never got a mix. I don't know what happened to the tape. I have a very *bad* cassette of it somewhere. Lou Ann doing "You'll Lose a Good Thing," Robert doing that Lil' Son Jackson song "Sugar Mama," which is kind of a mambo—"Sugar mama, sugar mama, where'd you get your sugar from?" Catman sang something. It was all very, very crude. We'd use Catman a lot and play with him and pay him as a member of the band, not necessarily with Robert, but mostly with stuff Freddie and I would do.

RAY THE SPADE

Mike: Another interesting character was Ray Cleveland, who called himself Ray the Spade. He played bass with us from time to time. He had been in Reverend Filmore's Swinging Flames with Freddie. Ray always wore either an Afro or Beatle wig and would always be elaborately decked out often in a full-length fur coat, even in the heat of summer. I remember going to Denny's with him and [the stripper-singer] Bubbles Cash. We got some looks, especially due to the fact that Ray had split-beaver shots from *Hustler* magazine pasted all over his guitar case. Ray lived with his grandmother in Como along with what seemed like dozens of children running around. I remember smoking pot with Gramma, whose place was decorated with beaded curtains and blacklight zodiac posters.

CURLY "BAREFOOT" MILLER

IIIIIIIIIIIIIIIIIIIIIIIII

Freddie: He would dance barefooted on a Coke box and have a microphone next to the Coke box. He would keep rhythm and dance and sing and play. He'd play drums. He'd play piano, tell the nastiest jokes you ever heard in your life. He was almost 80 years old, and had all this energy. I asked him one time, "You play piano so beautifully and you're this old, how do your hands . . . ?" He said, "Well, I go by the cedar bush out in my yard and I get the berries off the cedar bush and I grind them up and I rub them in my hands. And I can *plaaay*." He had his home remedy for arthritis and stuff.

Mike: "Y'all didn't get it, but she did!" That was one of his punch lines.

FINNEY-MO

IIIIIIIIIIIIIIIIIIIIIIIIIIIIIIIIII

Freddie: He dressed up like a woman, came out there and told some nasty jokes, and he had on this party dress. And every now and then, if he wasn't getting enough laughs, those underwear would just hit the floor. He'd say, "Oh, I'm sorry, I'm sorry." He had it so he could drop them any time he wanted to. He was just the funniest man.

Mike: Finney-Mo would come in in drag sometimes and do Moms Mabley. Then a real drag queen, Jerry Walker, "Sissy Jerry," that Rudy Ray Moore produced a record on, showed up.

JERRY WALKER

IIIIIIIIIIIIIIIIIIIIIIIIIIIIIIIIIIIIIIIIIIIIIIII

Freddie: Jerry Walker. She or he or whatever you want to call it, singing "I Love the Life I Live."

Mike: It's a thing, you know. Little Richard came outta that, and Esquerita and Bobby Marchan, down in New Orleans. They're all part of the culture.

Freddie: Jerry Walker used to say you could tell he was a man, but it was so obvious, he'd say, "What God didn't give me, Goodyear did."

Mike: Jerry was talking about his recipe for douche: alum, LSD, and Colonel Sanders fried chicken. He'd say, "Alum make it tight, LSD make it out of sight, and Colonel Sanders make it finger-lickin' good." I heard he got killed in a dope deal, but Rudy Ray Moore told me his boyfriend killed him.

TORO

Freddie: Toro would come in from time to time. And he'd eat light bulbs. He was huge, and he just screamed. It was like he came out of the jungle or something. Man, it was just—he was crazy, wasn't he, Mike?

Mike: Yeah, he had huge feet.

Freddie: He didn't say much, he'd say, "Get me a light bulb, man." "Get me some light bulbs." And he would eat one, and pretend like he was choking. And he'd spit out that glass. He's screaming and glass and shit is blowing out of his mouth. Women screaming and running out the door. It was all part of the act. I don't know if he was really bleeding or not.

Mike: He came in one night [to Tack's Fun House downtown] and started dancing this crazy Ubangi dance, and he got a big bowl of pork rinds, crushed them up, put lighter fluid on them, then he screamed at the top of his lungs, still dancing. Robert lit a cigar off his [flaming] breath. Then he ate a light bulb. For his finale, he'd start spitting up blood. Women would be running out the door, freaking out.

Jackie: People would be running out of the place screaming in terror.

Sumter: He was a geek. I met him at the Glass Key one night. He was eating light bulbs and spitting blood for $10.

AND A SUPPORTING CAST OF CHARACTERS

Jackie: There were definitely some characters. One day, somebody came up and said, "Chuck Berry's in the house!" And we're like, "What? No, get outta here!" This guy walks in, and he could have passed—he looked like Chuck Berry. And he's carrying a guitar case and it's a Gibson guitar case, and he takes it out and he's got a cherry-red 335, and puts it on. He's left-handed. He went by Chuck Berry Jr.

Freddie: There was a constable, he'd come in in full dress with his badge and his gun, and he'd sit in, play some cool John Lee Hooker stuff. Bobby Gilmore would come and play with us from time to time. King Earl would come in and sit in.

Sumter: King Earl was a shade-tree mechanic.

King Earl (above) and Bobby Gilmore.

25

BLOW YOUR SOCKS, DADDY CHOPS, GET DOWN!
★ ★ **NOW APPEARING** ★ ★

IN PERSON

ROBERT EALEY
AND HIS

FIVE CARELESS LOVERS

★ ★ ★ ★ ★ ★ ★ ★ ★ ★
**SEE ROBERT DO HIS FAMOUS
CHAIR DANCE, AND
DON'T MISS ANOTHER
NIGHT OF BLUES HOO-DOO !!**
CALL US: 926-1331 — 926-3856

LONE STAR PRINTING CO., FORT WORTH, TEXAS

CALLING ALL BLUES
★ **IN PERSON** ★

ROBERT
EALEY
AND HIS BAND

WEEKENDS AT THE
BLUEBIRD
FORT WORTH ★ 737 – 0433

  **ASK A
BLUEBIRD
CUSTOMER**

LONE STAR PRINTING CO., FORT WORTH, TEXAS

HAVE YOUR NEXT SOCIAL AT THE

NEW
BLUEBIRD
NIGHT CLUB

CORNER OF HORNE & WELLESLEY
★ **FORT WORTH** ★

GRAND OPENING
MARCH 4 - 5

IN PERSON
FRIDAY   SATURDAY

 **ROBERT EALEY
BLUES BAND**

★ ★ ★ ★ ★ ★ ★ ★ ★ ★

LONE STAR PRINTING CO., FORT WORTH, TEXAS

ROCK AWAY ALL YOUR BLUES
★ **THE**
CARELESS LOVERS

WITH
ROBERT EALEY
★ ★ ★ ★ ★ ★ ★ ★ ★ ★
STILL COOKIN' IN TOWN:

NEW BLUE BIRD CLUB
FRIDAY + SATURDAY
9:00 to 2:00
CR. HORNE + WELLESLEY

LONE STAR PRINTING CO., FORT WORTH, TEXAS

POSTERS

[Freddie Cisneros designed the band's hard cardboard posters, suitable for stapling on telephone poles, and did posters for other bands, too.]

Freddie: My dad was a commercial artist and sign painter. I knew a lot about letterpress, which is the old style of making posters. I knew a little bit about sign painting and reproduction artwork. My dad had used Lone Star Printing, and I knew those people, how posters got made, the process. Most musicians have this self-promotion thing happening. It's just part of the deal. You don't want to be John Smith. You want to be *Rockin'* John Smith.

BEYOND THE BLUE BIRD

Mike: We played Everybody's Talking, Daddy-O's, The HOP. We played a bunch of blues joints, place on Rosedale, we played there Sunday afternoons, it would always be hopping, place in Stop Six, on Evans Avenue at Sugar Hill, which was next door to a couple pretty swanky after-hours clubs, the Flamingo and the Eldorado. You could drink all night. They had organ trios playing there, and this guy named Little Timmy Sims, kind of a little sissy organ player, he was really good. They'd serve you liquor in coffee cups and pretty much anything you wanted. There'd be gambling in the back. Played a lot of gambling-front places, and after hours.

We played some club somewhere around Sherman and got stiffed by the owner. Ralph and Robert, they both had a gun. They were banging in the guy's door and shit to get our money. We played in Austin a couple of times, the Abbey Inn, Soap Creek.

THE RECORDING OF *ROBERT EALEY AND HIS FIVE CARELESS LOVERS: LIVE AT THE NEW BLUE BIRD* (BLUE ROYAL)

[In 1972, the band made their first and only album, a live recording of a Saturday night at the New Blue Bird Nite Club, co-produced by Stephen Bruton and T Bone Burnett.]

Sumter: Stephen [Bruton] and T Bone [Burnett] had been playing together off and on for years, and I'd played with him some, too. I've known him since the eighth grade. T Bone's mother owned the Taj Mahal apartments not too far from where we grew up, on Sanguinet. We discovered that she had a swimming pool, and Stephen took quick advantage of that, and we all became friends.

T Bone had been into recording, producing stuff. His mother bought him Sound City Studios. He took equipment from the studio, put it on the pool table and taped it there.

Mike: Stephen and T Bone were the producers and engineers on it [assisted by musical friends Lindsey Holland, Roscoe West, and David Ferguson]. This guy Charles Stewart was a recording guy. He may have been the money. There was some money guy they all knew. T Bone's big claim to fame was playing drums for the Legendary Stardust Cowboy and recording him. I knew [Stephen] from the store, then he went to Woodstock for a while and hooked up with all those guys from The Band and Jim Colegrove, and he came back and was hanging out. I don't know how, or who, but somebody decided to record the Five Careless Lovers.

"I'm not really excited about that recording, mainly because I wasn't very good back then. I was just learning. But it is what it is. It's a document, and a lot of people have fond memories of that time and place in Fort Worth."

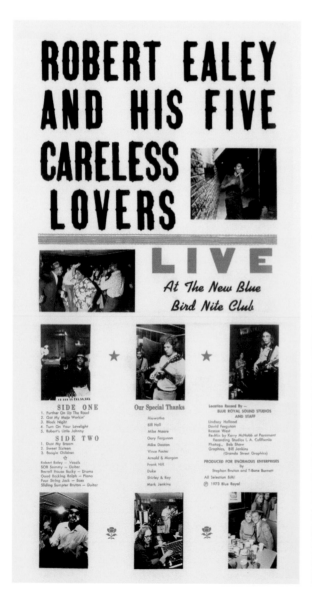

Sumter: It was a stormy fuckin' night. There was more electricity in the air that night coming out of them clouds, it was electric. You walked in and your hair stood up. And there was a sign that lit up on the wall without being plugged in. Eerie.

Freddie: I think we got an extra five bucks that night.

Mike: My first groupie experience. The place was packed. and it was fun. Everybody got real drunk. Ted Tucker got busted that night. He and Jim Yanaway left the Blue Bird and got stuck on a railway track in Ted's big Oldsmobile and a train came by and knocked the door off. Ted stashed a bag of pot behind a pole near the track. A cop heard Ted tell Jim: "Remember the third pole," and put two and two together.

Sumter: A guy in Arlington did the mixing and somehow one of the tapes got lost. Never found it. "Woke Up This Morning" was on it. I thought it was the better of the two [tapes], more jump blues involved in it.

We were gonna put out an album, a thousand copies. They were all numbered, or the first few hundred were numbered. I had [numbers] 1, 2, and 3 for a long time. It only cost a hundred dollars. Cheapo production. [The album cover] was just a piece of paper. We were cutting new ground. It was good to get an album out. I never had made a record before.

We sold them all.

Freddie: It wasn't like a hit record or anything.

Mike: I don't know if they were trying to make folk art or what. I'm not really excited about that recording, mainly because I wasn't very good back then. I was just learning. But

it is what it is. It's a document, and a lot of people have fond memories of that time and place in Fort Worth.

THE ART CROWD AND HIGH SOCIETY

||||||||||||||||||||||||||||||||||||||||||||||||||||||||||||||||||||||

Mike: T Bone and Stephen and Sumter, they all put one foot in the art crowd and one foot in the beer joints.

Jackie: Didn't Channel 13 come out and film? There was already some stuff like that going on.

Mike: We would play society events, play at the museum.

Jackie: Parties at Rivercrest [Country Club].

Mike: At one of those Rivercrest gigs, in the middle of a song, Robert goes up to some matronly white woman, gets right up in her face and goes, "I *know* you got the blues!"

Sumter: Robert was great. But sometimes, Robert would start talking to the crowd and you could see their eyes glaze over. You know, he'd do one of his rap things. It worked good at the Black clubs, but at the white clubs, they didn't know what the fuck he was talking about.
    He would laugh after everything he said.

I learned a lot from Robert. He said, "If someone really digs what you're doing, walk the table."

Jackie: We'd bring all of our hoodlum friends with us [to private parties the band played], and they'd be stealing the liquor.

Mike: Julie Newmar was hanging out at the Blue Bird for a while. For a short time [tabloid socialite] Priscilla Davis was coming around. Stephen brought all the Kristofferson band. [Stephen Bruton had become country singer-songwriter Kris Kristofferson's guitarist.] Apparently, Robert Crumb showed up there one night after I was

gone and did a little comic strip about it. It's called *R. Crumb Draws the Blues*. It's got a little Blue Bird segment. His comment was the band was too fuckin' loud, he had to leave.

Freddie: I think it had a lot to do with half the band was white. We started bringing *our* friends as well as playing for the crowd there. And it just kind of took. It was a thing. I never saw a fight between a Black guy and a white guy or a Mexican or anybody. It was always a Black guy fighting a Black guy or a white guy fighting a white guy. I never saw any crossover there. That was off-limits. The cops would come in there all the time trying to find something that we were doing wrong. They never could figure it out that we were just having fun, and people were there to hear the music and have a beer. It was just as simple as that.

T-BONE COMES TO THE NEW BLUE BIRD

Mike: I was driving to my gig at Tack's Fun House downtown, right by the projects, and this guy was out in the street, yelling, signaling, "Hey! Hey! Hey! Hey! Hey!" I pulled over and it was this guy I knew from the Blue Bird [Nathan Lewis]. "Hey, man, I want you to meet somebody." "Who is that?"

"Just come on." T-Bone Walker was sitting out on this guy's stoop, drinking Budweisers in the projects with his godson.

Sumter: We're playing at the Blue Bird, and I get a call from Nathan Lewis about T-Bone [coming to visit him in Fort Worth], and I said, "Sure, when he gets in town, have him call me." I went to the [record] store, and this motherfucker on the phone said, "Hey, Sumter. I want to talk to you about it." Two words out of his mouth, and I could tell it was T-Bone Walker. He comes down to the Blue Bird that night. He was staying with the Coopers. Bob and Maude Cooper were their names. They were his best friends. From the Jim [Hotel]. They introduced him to [his wife] Vida Lee. She worked at the Jim as a hostess.

I said [to the band], "T-Bone Walker's coming out," and Jackie looks at me and says, "Aw, you're crazy." And I said, "When T-Bone gets here, play 'Reconsider, Baby.'" As soon as I said that, I turned my head, and he's coming in the front door. He ended up playing the guitar a bunch that night, but he'd had that stroke, so that guitar ate him up. I had my big guitar, my T-Bone Walker model No. 12 Gibson, so he switched over to piano, and played great. He'd been playing piano in Europe. Because of the stroke, he couldn't bend the [guitar] strings. He was a little man, 5'6", maybe.

Black folks out there couldn't believe [it was] T-Bone. One old guy who was there every night, he was a tough customer.

Trailblazer of the modern electric blues guitar, Aaron T-Bone Walker visits Fort Worth kinfolk including godson Nathan Lewis (bottom left); and with Sumter Bruton (top row, second from right) and Fort Worth Press *reporter Pete Gordon (bottom right).*

He cursed like a sailor. He made T-Bone show him his driver's license. T-Bone had a great time, but he got so drunk, he couldn't make it back the next night. I had my tape player ready to go, and he called in sick. He stayed in. But he came over to my house the next day, Sunday. I played him all these 78s he hadn't heard—he'd heard the A-side, but never heard the B-side. He had total recall. "I raised that one, that's so-and-so. That's Maxwell Davis, that's Luther McDaniels" and all that. So we got over there and smoked pot all day. He was a pot smoker then. [He'd] get it, and never hand it away.

I played him all his records. One of my ex-girlfriends showed up and gave him a rubber [therapy] ball. "Keep using that." He said, "Well, I'm ready for some Mexican food today." We went to The Original to eat, and that's the last time I ever saw him. He died not too long after that.

The New Blue Bird in the early evening when the venue functioned as a neighborhood hangout before the band started playing.

> "Two words out of his mouth, and I could tell it was T-Bone Walker. He comes down to the Blue Bird that night."

GUNS

||||||||||||||||||||

Freddie: Well, we had to dodge a few bullets, man.

Jackie: I got robbed at Mable's loading my van. I knew the guys. When I worked at Zeke's Fish and Chips, they were the kids that we used to have to chase out of there. I recognized them. I just took most of the money out of my wallet and handed it to them.

Freddie: Mike and I were playing at the Silver Dollar one night, and after we got through, we went out the back door and loaded up and got in the car, started it— nothing. I had to look under [the hood]. No battery.

Sumter: One night, two Black guys came in [to Mable's Eat Shop], and they were fucked up. They didn't have any PCP, they were just fuckin' drunk out of their minds, and they started giving people shit in the crowd. These guys were bugging the shit out of everybody, going table to table, just being mean. And there was a little old man, porkpie hat, coat and tie, and he was sitting right in front of us, at a table by himself. These guys start jerkin' with him, and he said, "Get away from me, boy!" One of the guys said, "What you gonna do about, it, old man?" You know, typical shit. "You get away from me. I'll shoot you." The guy said, "Ah, you!" Well, the little old man pulled out a gun and shot the motherfucker right there, three feet in front of me. That motherfucker dropped like a bag of cement, and then he went over in the corner and sat down. He was in shock, I guess.

The Five Careless Lovers and Robert Ealey at Mable's Eat Shop, where the band came together and built a following.

"When the ambulance came, before they got him in, he jumped off the gurney and went running down the street. There were a couple of white cops there, and one of them said, 'Do you want to go get him?' And the other one said, 'Nah, fuck it,' and everybody went home."

Jackie: This smaller, dapper guy was dressed in a suit, and these country guys came in, wearing overhauls, and raising a ruckus, and pushing people around. The gun came out; he put it on the table and just sat there. And I think one of them must have invaded his space or something, so we heard a gunshot. Everybody hit the floor. The guy was shot. In the shoulder. We went to various places to hide. I think Bucky was in the ladies' room, and I was back in the kitchen because there was a beer cooler that you could get behind.

Mike: When the shooting started, I was pulled into the ladies' room by a large African-American lady, joining seven or eight other women of similar size. We were all jammed in this tiny room together. I seem to recall one woman firing up a joint.

Sumter: The old man put his gun back in his pocket, walked out the front door and was gone. The cops got called. It took about twenty minutes for them to get there, because it was a n----r shooting—not much hurry about this thing, they take care of themselves. Cops came in, ambulance comes in, and they start to strap him in. The motherfucker gets a second hurrah, tears the straps all upside down, jumps off the stretcher, and runs off.

Jackie: When the ambulance came, before they got him in, he jumped off the gurney and went running down the street. There were a couple of white cops there, and one of them said, "Do you want to go get him?" And the other one said, "Nah, fuck it," and everybody went home.

Sumter: We quit. We all left. We all went home. I asked Robert, "What happened?" "Oh, that old boy, he's out from Burleson somewhere, he was just drunk." "What happened to the old man?" "He lived up the corner, he just went home." And that was it! There was no report filed. So, I went home and was like, "Whoa! That guy was *shot*." He had to have gone to the hospital sometime that night. The bullet lodged right about there [in his right shoulder].

Mike: That was about the only time. You were aware that people had guns and there'd be the occasional fight, but all in all, people were well-behaved and civil.

ON TO THE NEXT

||||||||||||||||||||||||||||||||||||||||||||||||||||||||

[By 1975, some of the Five Careless Lovers started to scatter. Mike Buck, Freddie, and Ralph, along with Lou Ann Barton, formed a side band, the Drifting Heartbreaks, behind singer M.C. Thomas, while Buck also started drumming behind stripper-entertainer Bubbles Cash, leading her band The Bucks.]

Sumter: Buck left; we kept going [as the Careless Lovers—minus the Five]. Danny Hukill

The reworked lineup of Careless Lovers perform for KERA television with Danny Hukill on drums and Craig Simecheck on keyboards, after the departure of Mike Buck and Good Rockin' Ralph Owens.

stepped right in. He and Freddie knew each other. Ralph got back into gospel. Ralph was a nice guy—grouchy, but nice. Freddie left after awhile. It was still me, Jackie, and [keyboardist Craig] Simecheck. Jackie left not long after that. Bud Johnson came in on guitar, he was a real good singer from South Louisiana. I hired [Jim] Colegrove to play bass. I was playing two or three different gigs a week. Everybody was. I was working at Tootsie's [with a four-piece]. Everybody was moving and grooving and changing things around. Blues had gotten real popular all of a sudden. Basically, it was Black joints and deb parties for the hip chicks on the west side— they knew about us, came out to the Blue Bird. All of a sudden, it became The Thing.

ROCK AWAY ALL YOUR BLUES
THE CARELESS LOVERS

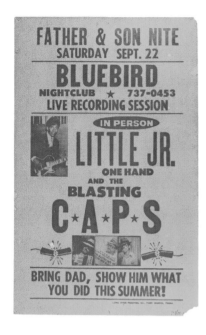

Freddie: There was a time in the mid '70s that I wasn't part of the band. It changed members a bunch after that. Jim Colegrove got in with Sumter [forming the Juke Jumpers]. Me and Cadillac [Johnson] and Craig Simecheck and Steven Springer had a band called Little Junior One Hand and the Blasting Caps and we got back and started playing with Robert later in the '70s.

[According to their official biography, the Juke Jumpers' first performance was in June 1977, with Jim Colegrove on bass and vocals, Sumter on guitar, Bud Johnson on guitar and vocals, and Buck on drums. Bud and Buck left the band before the end of the year, and Jim switched from bass to guitar, while adding Jackie Newhouse on bass with Mike Bartula on drums. Craig Simecheck, Jim Milan, and Johnny Reno would join later. The Juke Jumpers became the house band at the New Blue Bird Nite Club, often backing up Robert Ealey. Later iterations of the Juke Jumpers included drummer-singer Doyle Bramhall and Mike Judge.]

Mike: It was a split between Robert and Jackie and Sumter, and then me and Freddie and Ralph had this other band. We were a little frustrated with Robert's limitations. Although people loved him, he wouldn't try [to learn new material]. What he did was great, it seemed like we just grew apart, wanted to try something different. I don't think there was any real animosity. We backed up this guy, he was Ralph's cousin, R.L. Owens. And he was like a soul singer guy. He was really good. He did O.V. Wright. Freddie named him T.V. Owens. Lou Ann [Barton] started playing with that band.

[Freddie created a poster for the band, advertising the group as T.V. Owens and the Fabulous Erections.]

Jackie: My mother saw that poster and said, "Well, that's an interesting name."

[The band behind Robert functioned like a finishing school, with a steady stream of new players showing up, sitting in, developing chops, and sometimes even becoming part of the band. Saxophonist Johnny Reno started sitting in with the band in 1974 to become the newest Careless Lover.]

Johnny: I'd go to Freddie's on Wednesdays and he'd show me

> "What he did was great, it seemed like we just grew apart, wanted to try something different. I don't think there was any real animosity."

how to play sax, then I'd play what he taught me on the weekends at the Blue Bird without a microphone, for about a year, figuring out how to do it.

[Michael Pellecchia, a TCU grad with formal music training, showed up in the fall of 1974 joining Reno along with Freddie for a three-sax lineup, while Carney Bell—real name C.B. Scott—filled in on guitar for Freddie.]

Michael Pellecchia: Willis Johnson was still coming in from time to time [to play sax]. He had played with Ray Charles, and went way back with Robert. He did horn acrobatics. He would throw my horn into the air and catch it in between riffs. I had to lend him mine because his was usually in the pawn shop. When three of us were playing sax and coordinating riffs, Johnny Reno got us some rental outfits to look like a section. Ralph was showing up less and Craig was showing up more.

The Five Careless Lovers evolved into the Careless Lovers, as Johnny Reno (second from left) began playing with the band in 1974, later joined by Gerard Daily (second from right) and occasionally sax showman Willis Johnson (left). Darrell Nulisch (far right) honed his harmonica and singing chops sitting in with the band.

Craig Simecheck: I joined about 1974 or 1975. I was a really green blues piano player and lived next door to Freddie. He heard me practicing and loaned me a stack of blues piano 45s, mainly boogie-woogie. Ralph was still in the band but announcing that he might have to quit. I think his wife was pushing it. Freddie asked me to come out to the Blue Bird and sit in. I didn't think I was ready, but I did.

After the Careless Lovers, Freddie, Cadillac, Steve Springer and I started the Blasting Caps somewhere around 1976-77. I joined the Juke Jumpers in 1980. We were Robert's backup band and continued to play the Blue Bird a lot.

I helped form a group to allow Robert to reopen the club in his name [on March 4, 1977]. I did a lot of construction work on the bathrooms and all the fixtures. We got the lease in Robert's name and the crowds came back bigger than ever.

Michael Pellecchia: I played all Robert's gigs, including that memorable night of the Rolling Thunder Revue drop-in [T Bone Burnett brought Bob Dylan and his musical friends who were on tour to the Blue Bird one weekend in the spring of 1976]. The Smithsonian Folklife people came and said they were putting Robert in the Smithsonian. I wonder what became of that? During that period, the band name changed. I left for New York that fall.

Gerard Daily: I started sitting in at the Blue Bird during my last semester at TCU. Sumter and I were in Rhumboogie together, and in Boogie Uproar along with Mike Buck, John Austin, Bill Eagle, and Bud Johnson. In September of 1975 I enrolled at Tarrant County Junior College to take Automotive Mechanics. I already had a degree and various English courses so I took French and played in the stage band to get enough hours to be enrolled as a part-time student. I played baritone saxophone in the stage band, and TCJC let me take a horn home, so I played baritone at the Blue Bird. I sat in occasionally at the Blue Bird but not every weekend. I moved to Austin the summer of '77 and I had been there a few months when Mike called me and told me he had moved to Austin to play with the T-Birds.

Mike: I left for Austin in 1977 [to be a Fabulous Thunderbird]. Jackie left shortly after that [to join Stevie Vaughan's Triple Threat Revue alongside Johnny Reno, and then the first iteration of Double Trouble]. When we were playing over at Chicken in the Basket, they'd watch out for us, take us under their wing. You know, the people warmed up [to us]. They seemed to like it. After I left Fort Worth, there was some kinda stink in the papers, some woman complaining about white people taking over the neighborhood and the Blue Bird and all that.

BEING A CARELESS LOVER

||||||||||||||||||||||||||||||||||||||||||||||||||||||||||||||||||

Sumter: There were Black bands, and there were white bands, and they didn't mix much. Little Al and the Hi-Fi's were my favorite band. Louis Howard and the Red Hearts was another favorite; I used to go see C.L. Dupree play with them. They were a Black band that could play the white clubs. But it was pretty segregated still. There weren't any clubs where everybody could get together and play. Mable's Eat Shop became that club, and we were that band, mixing it up. And then we went across the street to the big house—the Blue Bird!

Freddie: That was my education, man. I don't think it'll ever be that way again because times have changed. Nowadays you'd get killed going in there. It was dangerous back then but not like now. You know what I'm saying?

Jackie: It was an undergrad school of the blues. I barely knew how to play when I started with these guys, and they taught me a lot: how to play, how to play with other people, how to act, how to carry yourself and . . .

Mike: How to listen.

Jackie: How to listen. That's really important. Kind of a nonverbal communication that musicians have.

Sumter: Robert and I just got along. He was a fantastic singer even though he didn't know the words to songs. One night he told me, "That makes no difference. B.B. King makes everything up." "He does?" "Yeah, every song is different." He would put on an act now and

"It was an undergrad school of the blues. I barely knew how to play when I started with these guys, and they taught me a lot: how to play, how to play with other people, how to act, how to carry yourself and … How to listen."

then where he started talking in ebonics—I understood every fucking word he said, know what I'm saying? He could make a long sentence short, leaving out some adjectives and adverbs. We never had an argument. We were friends. We worked together almost every weekend from '68 to '80. It was fun.

Mike: We were all young, and it was a very exciting time, getting exposed to this music that we'd never heard, or may have heard only a little bit. You know how segregated Fort Worth was. You wouldn't go to a Black club. There'd probably be no reason to. It wouldn't occur to you to go to one, but then you start hearing this stuff on KNOK and different stations. A lot of white kids were attracted to it. Delbert [McClinton] and all those guys were doing it long before us. You go back to Bob Wills' days.

I'm not sure what bringing a bunch of white people there accomplished other than bring us all a little closer together. I'm not sure I've learned yet. Still working on it.

We were just kids getting high and having a great time, man.

Freddie Cisneros

eventually moved to Houston to play with the Cold Cuts and front his own band, the Sheetrockers, before relocating to Prescott, Arizona, where he is a luthier who services Martin and Fender guitars, and occasionally performs.

Sumter Bruton

continued playing behind Robert, with the Juke Jumpers, until their breakup in 1990; on pickup gigs with Johnny B.; doing jazz and swing in the Rhumboogie ensemble and smaller combos; and collaborating with keyboardist Mike Price, all while working the counter of Record Town. He retired from Record Town when the store was sold and moved in 2018, and is retired from music.

Jackie Newhouse

plays bass for blues guitarist Alan Haynes, after a career playing with Stevie Ray Vaughan's Triple Threat Revue and Double Trouble, Anson Funderburgh and the Rockets, and the Leroi Brothers. He lives in Austin.

Mike Buck

*was the drummer
for the Fabulous
Thunderbirds,
co-founded the Leroi
Brothers, and played
with Doug Sahm in
the Texas Mavericks.
He co-owns
Antone's Record Shop
in Austin with his
wife, the guitarist
Eve Monsees, with
whom he plays drums
in Eve and the Exiles,
as well as with
several other bands.*

Good Rockin'
Ralph Owens

*returned to the church
and became
Reverend Ralph Owens.
He passed in 2006.*

Robert Ealey

*continued performing
and nurturing
young talent at the
New Blue Bird.
He died in 2001 after
a head-on collision
with a wrong-way
driver on a downtown
Fort Worth street.
Reverend Ralph testified
and played organ at
Robert's funeral.*

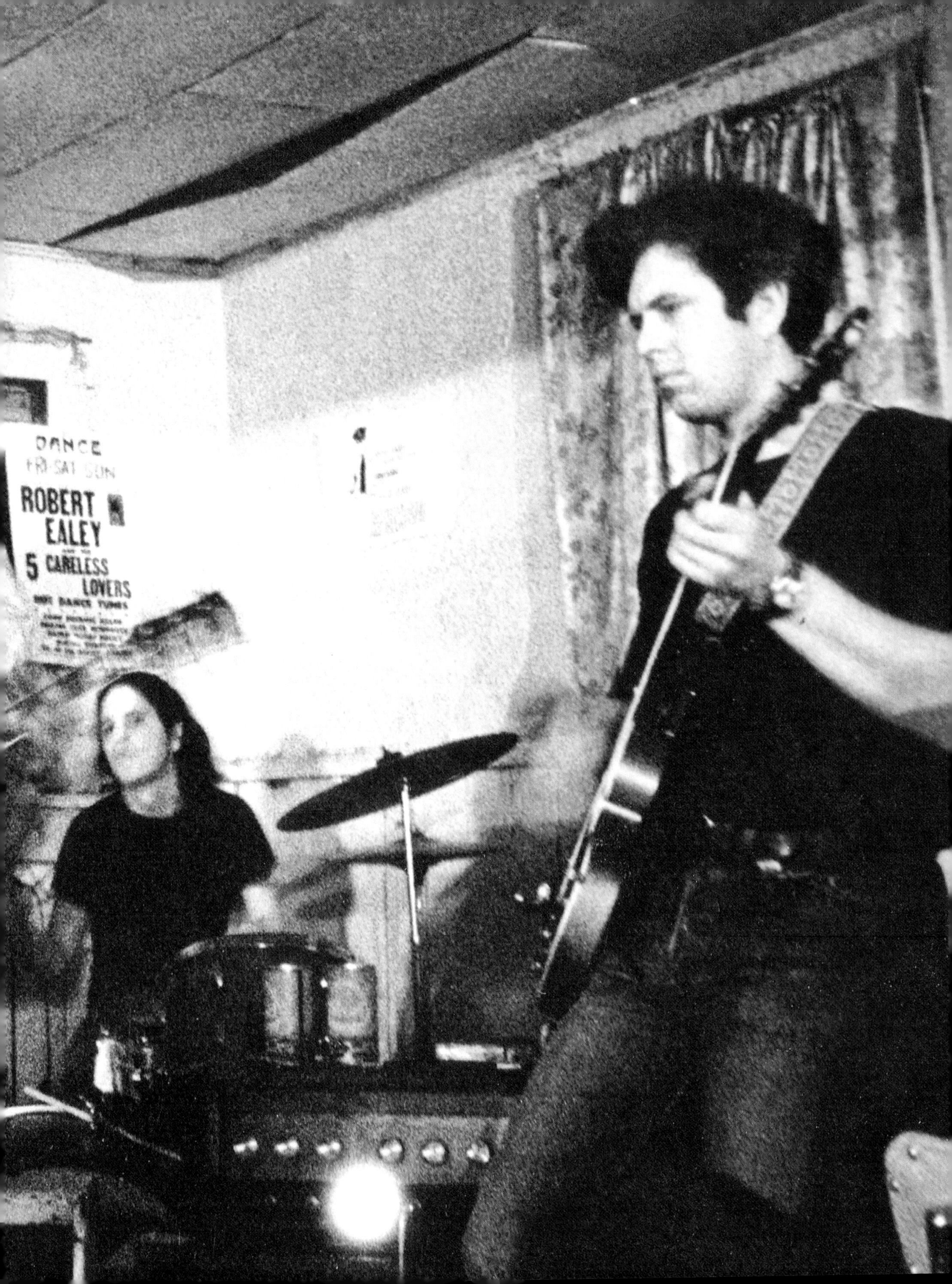
DANCE
FRI-SAT-SUN
ROBERT
EALEY
5 CARELESS
LOVERS

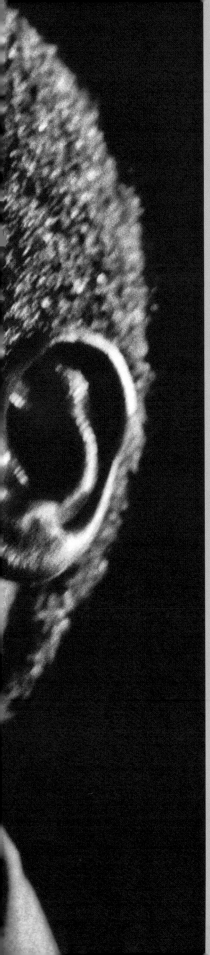

ACKNOWLEDGEMENTS

||||||||||||||||||||||||||||||||||||||||||||||||||||||||||||||||||||||||||||||

Additional Recording
Bill Mecke and Gerard Daily

Transcription
Jay Brakefield

Design & Production
Nancy McMillen

Copyediting
Cilla McMillen

Proofreading
Cilla McMillen and Anne Dingus

Copy Photography / Scanning
Wyatt McSpadden
Bill Mecke
Nancy McMillen
Bayou Fine Art Imaging

Special Thanks to:
Freddie Cisneros, Mike Buck, and Sumter Bruton,
for providing the photographs, posters,
and other images that help bring the words to life.

Thanks as well to Vince Foster, Bob Shaw, Bob Lukeman,
Jim Jones, Michael Pellechia, Jim Colegrove,
Susan Colegrove, Johnny Reno, and Christina Patoski
for their generous contributions to this project.

CLOCKWISE FROM TOP LEFT: *Young Mike Buck drumming at T.J.'s Chicken in the Basket; Stephen Bruton joining Sumter Bruton, Freddie Cisneros, and Good Rockin' Ralph Owens in a jam; Robert Ealey getting the drummer spotlight at Mable's Eat Shop; Freddie Cisneros practicing at home with his National reso-phonic guitar; Good Rockin' Ralph Owens and Smilin' Jackie Newhouse laying down the groove at Mable's.*

Robert Ealey getting down on bended knee while leading the Five Careless Lovers at Panther Hall, the storied music venue on Fort Worth's east side where country star Willie Nelson launched his career.

IMAGE CREDITS
||||||||||||||||||||||||||||||||||||||||||||||||||||||||||||